Pebble Plus

Halloween Fun

Black Cats

by Megan Cooley Peterson

Consulting editor: Gail Saunders-Smith, PhD

CAPSTONE PRESS
a capstone imprint

Pebble Plus is published by Capstone Press,
1710 Roe Crest Drive, North Mankato, Minnesota 56003
www.capstonepub.com

Library of Congress Cataloging-in-Publication Data
Peterson, Megan Cooley.
Black cats / by Megan Cooley Peterson.
pages cm.—(Pebble Plus. Halloween Fun)
Includes bibliographical references and index.
Summary: "Simple text and full-color photographs describe black cats and Halloween"—Provided by publisher.
ISBN 978-1-4765-2181-7 (library binding)
ISBN 978-1-4765-3492-3 (eBook PDF)
1. Halloween—Juvenile literature. 2. Black cats—Juvenile literature. I. Title.
GT2965.P47 2014
394.2646—dc23 2013005730

Editorial Credits
Jeni Wittrock, editor; Heidi Thompson, designer; Wanda Winch, media researcher; Laura Manthe, production specialist

Photo Credits
Alamy: Kathy Wright, 5; The Art Archive at Art Resource: CCI, 9; The Bridgeman Art Library: Archives Charmet/Private Collection/Savely Dezso, K., 11; Capstone Studio: Karon Dubke, 19, 21; Corbis: Blend Images/John Lund, 7, PoodlesRock, 13; Dreamstime: Lachertenok, 17, Vitaliy Rozhkov, Halloween icons; Shutterstock: Brberrys, cover, olga.lolipops, border, V, 15

Note to Parents and Teachers

The Halloween Fun set supports social studies standards related to holidays and culture. This book describes and illustrates black cats and Halloween. The images support early readers in understanding the text. The repetition of words and phrases helps early readers learn new words. This book also introduces early readers to subject-specific vocabulary words, which are defined in the Glossary section. Early readers may need assistance to read some words and to use the Table of Contents, Glossary, Read More, Internet Sites, and Index sections of the book.

Printed in the United States of America in North Mankato, Minnesota.
032013 007223CGF13

Table of Contents

Fearsome Felines

Dead leaves crunch under your feet as you trick-or-treat on Halloween. Suddenly a black cat darts in front of you. Hiss!

Black cats have scared people for hundreds of years. They arch their backs. Their big eyes glow. The black cat is a popular Halloween symbol.

Witches and Black Cats

In the 1500s and 1600s,
people believed that some
women had magical powers.
They were called witches.
Some witches had black cats.

Many people feared witches and their cats. They believed cats held a witch's spirit. A witch's cat could even put spells on people.

People also thought witches
could turn into black cats.
They told tales of witches
and cats flying on broomsticks.

Black Cat Features

A black cat's body is perfect for roaming at night. Its pupils grow wider at night. Wide pupils let in more light. Glowing eyes also help them see in low light.

A black cat's dark coat
blends in with the shadows.
It slinks quietly through alleys
and over fences with soft pads
on its paws.

Black Cats Today

Today we know that black cats are not evil. It is a superstition that they cause bad luck. In England and Japan, it is good luck to spot a black cat!

千万両

Black Cat Ring Toss

Tricks are fun on Halloween, but so are treats! Invite your friends over for a game of ring toss. Any player whose ring lands around a black cat gets to eat the lollipop!

What You Need

scissors
black cellophane
lollipops
white chenille stems
black and green felt with sticky backing
black construction paper
glue
dry floral foam

To Make

1 Cut cellophane into squares with scissors. Wrap cellophane around each lollipop head. Secure with a chenille stem.

2 To make the cats' ears, cut triangles from the black felt. Remove the backing and stick to the top of the lollipop.

3 To make eyes, cut oval shapes from the green felt and stick to the face.

4 Cut long pieces from the construction paper to make whiskers. Glue to the cats' faces below the eyes. Then place the lollipop stems in the floral foam.

5 Bend chenille stems into rings. Twist the ends together, and toss the rings onto the lollipops.

Glossary

coat—an animal's hair or fur

pupil—the round, dark center of your eye that lets in light

spell—a word or words supposed to have magical powers

spirit—the soul or invisible part of a person that is believed to control thoughts and feelings

superstition—a belief that an action can affect the outcome of a future event

symbol—something that stands for something else

Read More

Armentrout, David and Patricia. *Kitty Care*. Let's Talk about Pets. Vero Beach, Fla.: Rourke Pub., 2011.

Braun, Eric. *The Truth about Witches*. Fairy-tale Superstars. Mankato, Minn.: Picture Window Books, 2011.

Landau, Elaine. *What Is Halloween?* I Like Holidays! Berkeley Heights, N.J.: Enslow Publishers, 2012.

Internet Sites

FactHound offers a safe, fun way to find Internet sites related to this book. All of the sites on FactHound have been researched by our staff.

Here's all you do:

Visit *www.facthound.com*

Type in this code: 9781476521817

Index

Word Count: 198
Grade: 1
Early-Intervention Level: 16